Digging Dinosaurs

By
Judy Nayer

Modern Curriculum Press

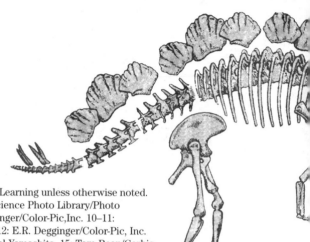

Credits

Photos: All photos © Pearson Learning unless otherwise noted.
Front cover: ©Mehau Kulyk/Science Photo Library/Photo
Researchers, Inc. 6: E.R. Degginger/Color-Pic,Inc. 10–11:
Jeff Gnass/The Stock Market. 12: E.R. Degginger/Color-Pic, Inc.
13: Brown Brothers. 14: Michael Yamashita. 15: Tom Bean/Corbis.
20: t.l. PhotoDisc, Inc.; b. E.R. Degginger/Color-Pic, Inc.
23: P.M. Grecco/Stock Boston. 32: ©Jean-Phillippe Varin/Photo
Researchers, Inc. 34: ©James L. Amos/Photo Researchers, Inc.
40: E.R. Degginger/Color-Pic, Inc. 41: Tom Smart/Gamma Liaison. 46: Rudi Von
Briel/PhotoEdit. 47: Nancy Jenkins/Denver Museum of Natural History/Gamma
Liaison.

Illustrations: 5, 7, 8–9, 16–17, 18, 19, 20, 21, 22, 24, 25, 26, 27, 28, 29, 30, 31, 33, 35,
36–37, 38, 39: Gary Torrisi.

Cover and book design by Agatha Jaspon

Printed in the United States of America
10 11 12 13   07 06

Modern
Curriculum
Press

Pearson Learning Group

1-800-321-3106
www.pearsonlearning.com

CONTENTS

CHAPTER 1

What Are Dinosaurs?

Imagine looking up and seeing a big reptile's head rise high above the trees. Imagine this reptile bending down its long neck to look at you. Imagine an animal as big as a truck stomping down the street. This is what you might see if dinosaurs lived on Earth today.

Dinosaurs were a group of animals that used to roam the earth. However, they have been gone for a long time. They lived millions of years ago before there were any people.

Apatosaurus

Komodo dragon

The name *dinosaur* means "terrible lizard." When people first found dinosaur bones, they thought they were the bones of a giant lizard. They thought that such a big lizard would be "terrible" and fierce.

Like lizards, dinosaurs were reptiles. They laid eggs, and they had skin that was scaly. Most reptiles today, like the Komodo dragon, walk on four legs. Their legs spread out from the sides of their bodies. Many dinosaurs also walked on four legs.

However, dinosaurs were different from the reptiles we know today. They were much bigger. Many of them also walked on two long legs, just like people.

There were hundreds of different kinds of dinosaurs. Some were big, some were small. Some were fast, others were slow. Some were fierce meat eaters. Other dinosaurs were gentle and ate plants.

Thescelosaurus

Dinosaurs lived all over the world for about 165 million years. However, not all of them lived at the same time. Many kinds lived millions of years apart from each other.

During the time that dinosaurs lived, the earth went through many changes. As millions of years passed, the earth became drier, then wetter. Different kinds of plants grew. The kinds of dinosaurs changed along with the earth. As a group of dinosaurs slowly died off, a new group took its place.

The years during which dinosaurs lived are divided into three time periods. Each period is based on changes in climate and plant life.

THE AGE OF THE DINOSAURS

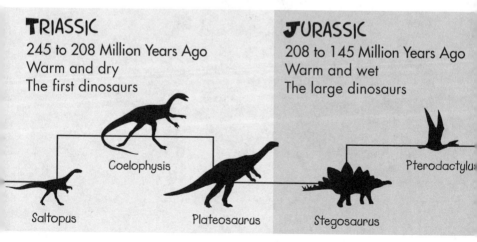

TRIASSIC
245 to 208 Million Years Ago
Warm and dry
The first dinosaurs

Coelophysis

Saltopus

Plateosaurus

JURASSIC
208 to 145 Million Years Ago
Warm and wet
The large dinosaurs

Pterodactylus

Stegosaurus

All the dinosaurs were gone long before there were people to see them. So, how do we know so much about dinosaurs?

Did You Know?

It is hard to imagine how long ago dinosaurs lived. Think of the years as steps. Imagine that one step is 1,000 years. To go back to the time of the dinosaurs, you would have to walk enough steps to cover 30 miles!

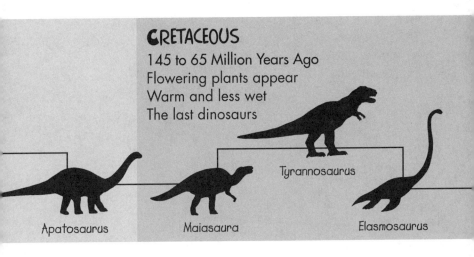

CRETACEOUS
145 to 65 Million Years Ago
Flowering plants appear
Warm and less wet
The last dinosaurs

Tyrannosaurus

Apatosaurus   Maiasaura   Elasmosaurus

How Do We Know About Dinosaurs?

Everything we know about dinosaurs comes from what they left behind. They left bones, teeth, footprints, skin prints, and even eggs. These remains are called fossils.

How were the fossils made? When some dinosaurs died, they were covered with sand and mud. Their bodies rotted away. Bones and other hard parts were left. Over millions of years the bones, sand, and mud turned to stone. The bones became fossils.

Dinosaur bones in the ground

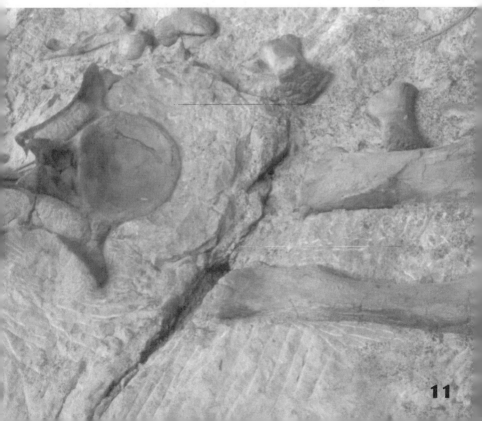

For millions of years the fossils stayed buried in the ground. Then people began to find them.

In 1822, Mary Ann Mantell found some giant fossil teeth near her home in England. They looked like the teeth of a lizard, only ten times bigger.

Mrs. Mantell's husband, Dr. Gideon Mantell, was a scientist. He thought the teeth looked like those of an iguana, a kind of lizard. So,

Iguana

he named the mystery animal *iguanodon* (ih GWAHN uh dahn). The name means "iguana tooth."

The iguanodon turned out to be a plant eater that lived in herds. On each hand it had a sharp spike it probably used to protect itself.

After that, more and more giant fossils were found in England and in other countries. Scientists said they all belonged to a group of giant reptiles that lived millions of years ago. They named them dinosaurs.

Dinosaur hunter

Ever since, scientists have been looking for dinosaur fossils. They dig the fossil bones out of rock. Then they fit the dinosaur bones together like a puzzle to make a whole skeleton. From the skeleton they can tell how big the dinosaur was, what shape it was, and how it moved.

Fossil teeth tell us what the dinosaurs ate. Sharp, pointy teeth belonged to meat eaters. Odd-shaped or flat teeth came from plant eaters.

Dinosaur display in the
New York Museum of Natural History

Fossil skin shows that dinosaurs had scaly skin like reptiles. Fossil footprints show the shape of their toes. Fossil eggs tell how baby dinosaurs were born.

With each new dinosaur found or uncovered, we learn more about dinosaurs and their world.

Paleontologist Susan Lamb shows fossil footprint.

Did You Know?

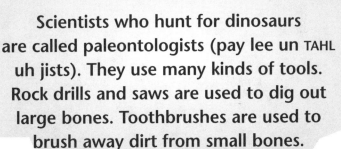

Scientists who hunt for dinosaurs are called paleontologists (pay lee un TAHL uh jists). They use many kinds of tools. Rock drills and saws are used to dig out large bones. Toothbrushes are used to brush away dirt from small bones.

CHAPTER 3

The First Dinosaurs

Iguanodon was the first animal identified as a dinosaur. However, it was not the first dinosaur that lived on Earth. Iguanodon lived about 140 million years ago. The first dinosaurs appeared about 245 million years ago.

We know these dinosaurs were the first because of fossils found in layers of rock. The deepest layers of rock are the oldest. The layer of rock in which a fossil is buried tells about the age of the dinosaur.

When the first dinosaurs were alive, the world was much warmer and drier than it is now. At that time all of the earth's land was joined together. The dinosaurs could roam all over the world.

Scientists think the first dinosaurs were small meat eaters. They walked and ran on two legs. They used their long tails for balance. They shared the world with many other kinds of reptiles.

Coelophysis
hunting

One of these early meat eaters was
Coelophysis (see loh FYS ihs). Coelophysis was
about the size of a deer. Because of its light
bones, Coelophysis could run fast.

Coelophysis was small but fierce. It had
sharp, pointy teeth. Its claws were sharp for
catching prey. Coelophysis ate anything it
could catch. Scientists think it hunted in packs
as wolves do today.

The first big dinosaur was Plateosaurus (plat ee oh SAWR us). Plateosaurus was a tall plant eater. It walked on all fours. It stood on its back legs to reach for food in the high trees.

Plateosaurus was only the beginning of the big dinosaurs. Over millions of years, many dinosaurs grew larger and larger.

Plateosaurus eating

Another early dinosaur was one of the smallest dinosaurs that scientists have found. Saltopus (SALT oh pus) weighed only 2 pounds (1 kg) and was about the size of a kitten.

Saltopus

Did You Know?

Crocodiles were some of the reptiles that shared the earth with the first dinosaurs. Crocodiles today look a lot like their distant relatives did millions of years ago.

The Plant Eaters

The biggest dinosaurs were a group of plant eaters. These giants had big bodies, small heads, and long necks and tails. They walked on all fours. They spent most of their time eating.

One of these giants was Apatosaurus (ah pat oh SAWR us). It was 70 feet (21 m) long. This was as long as 11 beds placed end to end. It was as heavy as six elephants. Footprints show that Apatosaurus moved in herds, looking for food.

Apatosaurus

Brachiosaurus

Brachiosaurus (brak ee oh SAWR us) was even bigger. It was almost twice as heavy as Apatosaurus. It was as tall as a building with four floors. For a long time, Brachiosaurus was thought to be the biggest and heaviest animal ever to walk the earth.

Today, bones of even bigger dinosaurs have been found. The heaviest so far is Ultrasaurus (UL truh sawr us). It may have weighed over 80 tons (7 t). That is as heavy as 59 cars.

One of the longest dinosaurs so far is Seismosaurus (SYZ moh sawr us), which means "earthshaking lizard." Scientists think it may have been 130 feet (42 m) long, which is about as long as four school buses parked end to end. No one has yet found enough bones to make a whole skeleton.

Howell Thomas, paleontologist, looks at dinosaur teeth.

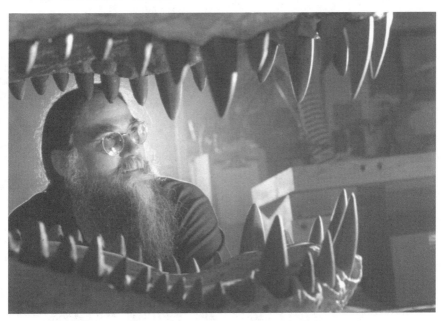

Many other dinosaurs lived at the same time as the giant plant eaters. One of them was a smaller plant eater named Stegosaurus (steg oh SAWR us). Stegosaurus had a big body, but its head was tiny. Its brain was only the size of a walnut.

Stegosaurus had a row of plates on its back. The plates may have helped heat up or cool down its body. Stegosaurus also had spikes on its tail. It could use its tail to protect itself.

Stegosaurus

Did You Know?

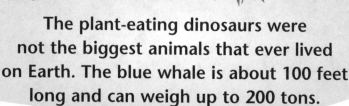

The plant-eating dinosaurs were not the biggest animals that ever lived on Earth. The blue whale is about 100 feet long and can weigh up to 200 tons.

The Meat Eaters

The meat eaters are the dinosaurs that many people think of when they hear the words *terrible lizards*. Most meat eaters walked on their two back legs. They hunted other dinosaurs. Some hunted alone. Others gathered in packs. In packs they could kill bigger dinosaurs.

Tyrannosaurus (tuh ran uh SAWR us) rex was one of the biggest of all meat eaters. It was 40 feet (13 m) long. This was as long as eight bathtubs set end to end. Its huge jaws were filled with sharp, six-inch teeth.

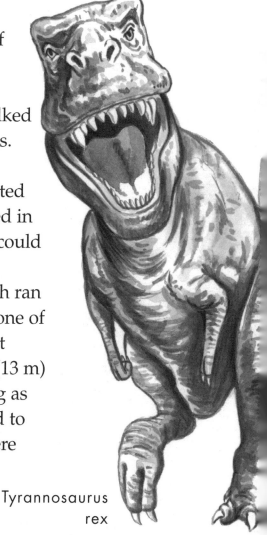

Tyrannosaurus rex

Not all meat eaters were big. Deinonychus (dye NAHN ih kus) was only about as long as a tiger. Even so, it was a fast and deadly killer. Its name means "terrible claw" for the sharp claw on each back foot. It used these claws to slash its prey.

By hunting in packs, a group of Deinonychus could attack big plant eaters. Deinonychus had a larger brain than many dinosaurs, too. With a large brain it may have been smart enough to plan attacks.

Deinonychus

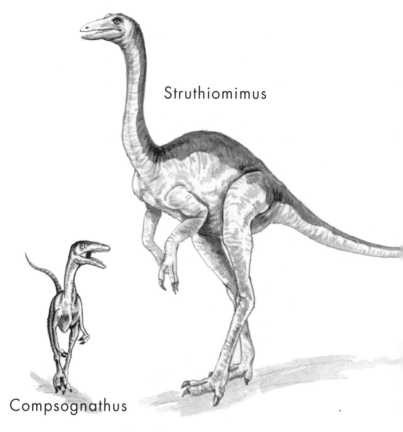

Struthiomimus

Compsognathus

Struthiomimus (STROOTH ee oh MYM us)
looked a lot like an ostrich without feathers.
It was one of the fastest meat-eating
dinosaurs. Struthiomimus ate insects, lizards,
and small mammals.

Compsognathus (kahmp SAHG na thus) was
one of the smallest meat eaters. It was not
much bigger than a chicken. Its small size
didn't stop it from hunting smaller lizards.

By the time meat eaters like Tyrannosaurus rex roamed the earth, the biggest plant eaters were gone. But many new kinds of smaller plant-eating dinosaurs took their place. Some were too slow to run away from enemies. They had to protect themselves in other ways.

Some dinosaurs had tough skin like armor. Another group of dinosaurs had horns. Triceratops (trye SER uh tahps) had three horns to scare off meat eaters. It had one on its nose and one over each eye. It also had a shield of bone to protect its neck.

Triceratops

Did You Know?

Tyrannosaurus rex could open its mouth wide enough to eat an animal as big as a bathtub. It was always losing its teeth. It grew new ones to take the place of any teeth that were lost.

Boneheads and Duckbills

Some dinosaurs had horns. Some had spikes along their backs or on their tails. Other groups of dinosaurs are known for the strange shape of their heads.

One group of dinosaurs with strange heads were the boneheads. Pachycephalosaurus (pak ih SEF uh loh SAWR us) had a cap of bone on its head that was nearly 10 inches (25 cm) thick. That's almost a one-foot layer of bone! Males may have fought by ramming each other with their heads as male sheep do today.

Pachycephalosaurus

A group of tall plant eaters that lived at the end of the age of dinosaurs are called duckbills. Duckbills had a flat beak that looked like a duck's bill. Big herds of them lived on the plains.

There were many different kinds of duckbills. Each kind had its own special head shape. Some duckbills had flat heads. Anatosaurus (ah NAT oh SAWR us) was one of them. It had more than 1,000 teeth for grinding the tough plants it ate. When its teeth wore down, new ones grew.

Anatosaurus

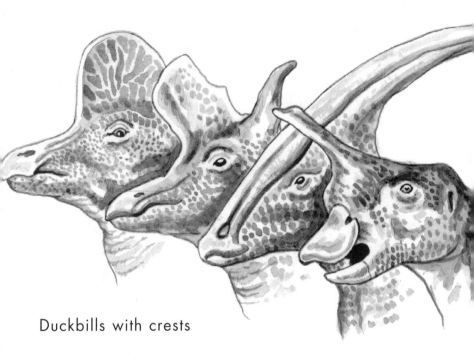

Duckbills with crests

Most kinds of duckbills had crests on their heads. A crest is a bony ridge that grows out from the head. It is usually long and narrow. Parasaurolophus (PAR uh sawr AHL oh fus) had a crest that was six feet long. That was as long as two yardsticks put together.

Some scientists think that duckbills blew through their noses to make loud sounds like a trumpet. Because the crest was hollow bone, it would make the sound louder. The duckbills may have used these sounds to signal each other.

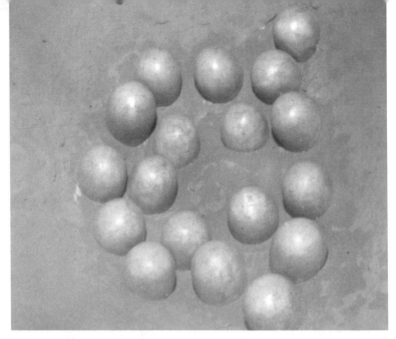

Fossils of Protoceratops eggs

Duckbills also have given scientists clues to how dinosaurs cared for their babies. Like all reptiles, dinosaurs laid eggs. Proof of this came in the 1920s. A nest was found with 30 eggs inside. The eggs were about the size of chicken eggs. The eggs belonged to a six-foot, plant-eating dinosaur called Protoceratops (PROH toh SER uh tahps).

Most reptiles today do not take care of their eggs or their babies. Scientists used to think dinosaurs were the same way. In 1978 a new discovery changed their minds.

A huge dinosaur nesting site was found in Montana. It belonged to a large kind of duckbill. Scientists called this duckbill Maiasaura (may yah SAWR uh), which means "good mother lizard."

Eggs and baby dinosaurs were found in the nests. Scientists also found young and adult dinosaurs nearby. This showed that parents stayed with their babies. They may have taken care of them and brought them food. This is how many birds care for their young. After all, the babies were no bigger than squirrels. They needed protection!

Maiasaura

When scientists began finding dinosaur eggs, they wondered why even the eggs of big dinosaurs were so small. The largest egg ever found was a Hypselosaurus (HIP sel oh SAWR us) egg. It was one foot long. The mother would have been nearly 40 feet (12 m) long.

John R. Horner with Hypsilophodont eggs

Scientists decided the eggs could not be too big or the shells would be too thick. If the shell had been too thick, the babies may not have been able to break the shell.

Did You Know?

Dinosaur names come from Greek and Latin words. Most names tell what a dinosaur looked like. Pachyrhinosaurus (pak ee ryne oh SAWR us) comes from *pachy*, which means "thick," and *rhino*, which means "nosed."

CHAPTER 7

Reptiles of the Sea and Air

While dinosaurs ruled the land, other reptiles filled the seas and skies. In the air were flying reptiles called pterosaurs (TER oh sawrz). They flew over the water on wings made of skin. They swooped down to the water to catch fish. Over the years different kinds and sizes of pterosaurs developed.

Pterosaurs flying

Pterodactylus and Quetzalcoatlus

Pterodactylus (ter oh DAK tih lus) was one of the smallest pterosaurs. It was only the size of a sparrow. Pteranodon (ter AN uh dahn) was one of the largest. Its wings spread 26 feet (8 m) across from tip to tip. Pteranodon had no teeth. It may have scooped up fish and swallowed them whole, as a pelican does.

The largest pterosaur was Quetzalcoatlus
(ket sahl koh AHTL us). It was the largest flying
animal ever. Its wingspan was 40 feet (13 m).
This is as big as that of a two-seater plane.
Quetzalcoatlus had no teeth. It fed on animals
that already died.

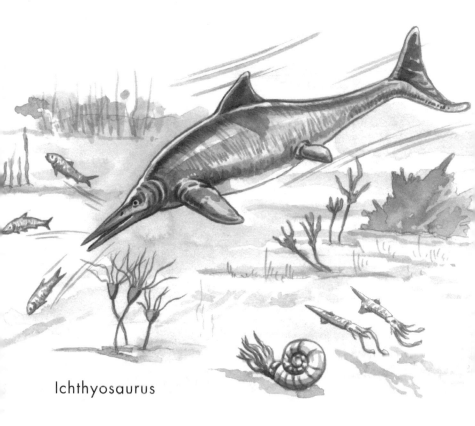

Ichthyosaurus

All kinds of reptiles lived in the warm sea in dinosaur times. Ichthyosaurus (ihk thee oh SAWR us) was one of the fishlike reptiles. It was a fast swimmer that looked something like a dolphin.

Archelon (AR keh lahn) was a giant sea turtle. It was about 12 feet (4 m) long, which is more than twice the size of the largest turtle today. Because it had weak jaws, it probably ate jellyfish.

Elasmosaurus (e LAZ moh SAWR us) was one of the long-necked sea reptiles. It used its flippers like paddles to swim through the sea. Elasmosaurus was 46 feet (14 m) long. It hunted sharks, squid, and smaller reptiles.

Plotosaurus (plah toh SAWR us) was a giant sea lizard. It had sharp teeth for catching prey.

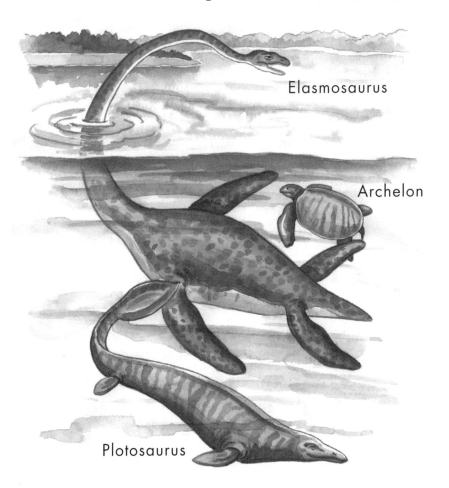

Elasmosaurus

Archelon

Plotosaurus

Brittle star

Scientists believe that when the dinosaurs died out some of the sea animals lived on. Some of them were animals we know today, such as brittle stars.

Did You Know?

Many people say they have seen a dinosaur-like animal with a long neck in Loch Ness, a lake in Scotland. Some people believe that the Loch Ness monster known as Nessie is really a kind of plesiosaur (PLEE see uh sawr), or sea reptile, like Elasmosaurus.

The End of the Dinosaurs

For nearly 180 million years, the dinosaurs ruled the earth. Then, about 65 million years ago, they all disappeared.

Scientists found that dinosaur bones were in old layers of rock, but not in new layers. They learned that not all the animals disappeared, yet the dinosaurs were gone. This was true all over the world. We don't know for sure what happened. But scientists have ideas.

Paleontologists look at rock layers.

Many scientists think that comets hit the earth 65 million years ago. Comets are huge balls of ice and rock that travel through space. If comets really did hit the earth, clouds of dust would have blown up into the air. These dust clouds would have blocked the sun's light. No plants could have grown. Plant-eating dinosaurs would have died because there was no food. Without plant eaters for food, the meat eaters would have died, too.

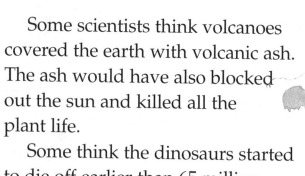

Some scientists think volcanoes covered the earth with volcanic ash. The ash would have also blocked out the sun and killed all the plant life.

Some think the dinosaurs started to die off earlier than 65 million years ago. The earth's temperature and weather had changed. The world was growing too cold for dinosaurs.

Maybe all of these things happened. Even though we are learning more about dinosaurs, there are still a lot of unanswered questions.

For example, what color were the dinosaurs? They may have been green or brown. Some may have been more colorful, as a lot of snakes, lizards, and birds are today. Maybe some had stripes or spots.

Were any dinosaurs warm-blooded, like mammals and birds? All of today's reptiles are cold-blooded. This means their blood is the temperature of the outside air. However, the skeletons of some dinosaurs show they may have been warm-blooded.

Are birds related to dinosaurs? Many scientists think birds are the dinosaur's cousins. Archaeopteryx (ahr kee AHP ter ihks) is the oldest bird that scientists have found. It has the same kind of skeleton as small meat-eating dinosaurs.

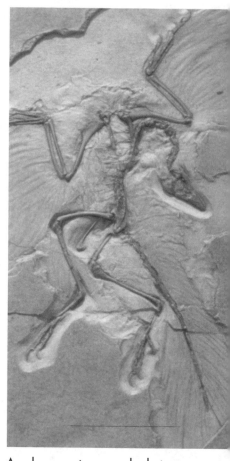
Archaeopteryx skeleton

What questions do you have about dinosaurs? We may never know all the answers. There is one thing we can be sure about. We will keep on digging. New information is being found all the time.

Paleontologists search for dinosaur bones.

Did You Know?

The only dinosaur ever found in Italy may help scientists tell if birds are related to dinosaurs. Some soft parts of the animal were left as well as bones. From the remains, scientists may be able to see if the animal breathed like birds or like reptiles.

GLOSSARY

crest (crest) a bony ridge that sticks out of the head of some animals

dinosaur (DYE nuh sawr) a reptile that lived on Earth's land from 245 to 65 million years ago

fossil (FAHS ul) an image found on a rock or the hardened remains of an animal or plant that was alive a long time ago

layer (LAY ur) a single thickness of something, such as rock, that is spread out over a surface

mammal (MAM ul) a warm-blooded animal, such as a lion, that has hair and feeds its young with milk from the female

prey (pray) an animal that is hunted and eaten

reptile (REP tyl) a cold-blooded animal, such as a lizard, that breathes with lungs and is covered with scales or hard plates

skeleton (SKEL uh tun) the bones inside a body

temperature (TEM pur uh chur) how hot or cold it is

volcano (vahl KAY noh) a mountain formed by hot, liquid rock that comes from inside the earth and explodes through a crack on the earth's surface